Growing up in
VICTORIAN BRITAIN

Sheila Ferguson

Head of the History Department
Peckham Girls' School, London

B.T. Batsford Ltd *London*

To all my friends at Peckham School

© Sheila Ferguson 1977

First published 1977
Reprinted 1979
Reprinted 1983

ISBN 0 7134 0281 4

Printed in Great Britain by
The Anchor Press Ltd, Tiptree, Essex
for the Publishers B T Batsford Limited
4 Fitzhardinge Street, London W1H 0AH

Frontispiece: **Children at a street fountain in
Battersea (photograph by Paul Martin)**

Acknowledgment

The Author and Publishers would like to thank the
following for their kind permission to reproduce
copyright illustrations:
   Ardea Photographics for fig 30; the Trustees of
the British Museum for figs 18, 22, 33; William
Gordon Davis for fig 19; the Geffrye Museum for
fig 20; A F Kersting for fig 9; London Borough
of Newham for fig 16; the Mansell Collection for
figs 2, 5, 6, 23, 25, 35-7, 40-2, 46-7; National
Monuments Record for fig 15; Radio Times Hulton
Picture Library for figs 7, 8, 17, 24, 26-9, 31-2,
34, 38, 43, 48-50, 55-8; the Science Museum for
figs 21, 45; the Tate Gallery for fig 11; the Victoria
and Albert Museum for the frontispiece and figs 1,
59, 60; and Weidenfeld and Nicolson Ltd for figs 4,
12-14 and 54.

Contents

The Illustrations

1 The Population Explosion

The growth and distribution of population
When Queen Victoria came to the Throne in 1837 more people lived and worked in the country than in the towns. Although her 'industrial revolution' had already earned Britain the title of 'the workshop of the world' most people, even the two million inhabitants of London, were not far from the countryside and children and their parents could get out of the towns fairly easily to walk in lanes and fields. By 1851, half the population were town-dwellers but 30 years later two-thirds lived in towns and only one-third in the country. So children growing up in the second half of the nineteenth century became increas-

1 The bridge across the River Lea at Walthamstow in about 1859 makes a peaceful village scene. Today it is a built-up London suburb

ingly unlikely to be country-dwellers and increasingly likely to live in an industrial town. From the Norman Conquest up to the middle of the eighteenth century, the southern and eastern counties had been the most populated parts of the country and the north and west the emptiest. This pattern was now practically reversed. The rapidly growing population was concentrating in the new industrial districts, the great coalfields of South Wales, the Midlands, Lancashire, Yorkshire, Tyneside and Clydeside. Apart from the London area, the south of England became comparatively unimportant.

Between 1801, when the first official census was taken, and 1851, the population of Great Britain had doubled and by 1901 it was well on the way to doubling itself again. The anxieties of the eighteenth-century writer Thomas Malthus that social

improvement would be cancelled out by a large population pressing on food supplies had been largely discounted by the mid-nineteenth century, since in spite of the increased numbers the standard of life was steadily rising. The reasons for this vast growth in population were many, but one of the most outstanding was the sharp fall in the death rate, especially the death rate of children. There was also a rise in the birth rate at the beginning of this period, but the major factor was that more babies were surviving. On average, women in the 1850s between the ages of 20 and 40 bore a child every three years. In some families a new addition to the household was more or less an annual event, which led one French traveller to compare the Victorian mother to a 'sitting hen'.

The infant death rate

Throughout most of the nineteenth century, 150 out of every 1,000 babies died during their first year, and it was only in the last few years of the century that serious efforts began to be made to prevent this fearful wastage of life. Babies were usually born at home and often no doctor attended the confinement. No doubt the mostly untrained midwives who delivered the babies were not all as dirty, drunken and irresponsible as Dickens' Sarah Gamp in *Martin Chuzzlewit*

2 The gin-sodden Mrs Gamp offers her card and services as a midwife to a young bride (from Charles Dickens' novel *Martin Chuzzlewit*)

but they had low standards of hygiene and were ill-equipped to cope with any except straightforward births. They went from case to case, unaware of the need to sterilize both themselves and their instruments. In consequence they spread 'childbed' fever among the mothers and infections that killed many of the babies. In 1902, the *Midwives Act* created the Central Midwives Board to register trained midwives; it became illegal for women to attend confinements 'habitually and for gain' unless they were certified midwives or working under the direction of a doctor. As a result of improved knowledge of hygiene and medicine, better training of midwives and a rising standard of living, fewer women could say 'I've had twelve children and buried six'.

Working mothers

One factor that affected the death rate among young children was whether or not their mothers went out to work, either employed in the textile mills of Lancashire and Yorkshire, the Potteries of Staffordshire or the fields of Lincolnshire or Norfolk. To contribute to the family income many women returned to work as soon as possible after their confinements, leaving their babies with unskilled baby-minders. Breast feeding had then to be abandoned and there was much ignorance about the need for hygiene and nutritional standards in artificial feeding. The baby-minders would often give a fretful baby a soothing syrup containing dangerous narcotics to keep it quiet. In the 1870s cheap, tinned, sweetened condensed milk came on the market and was widely used by poor families especially for children; it was, however, deficient in fats and vitamins and the government insisted that tins should be labelled with the information that condensed milk was unsuitable food for young children. Doubtless many who needed to heed the warning could not read, or even when they could would find the information unconvincing.

3 'What are the wild waves saying?' The delicate Paul Dombey, from Dickens' *Dombey and Son*, on the beach at Brighton (print by G. Every after a painting by Charles Nicholls)

The importance of mothers' personal care of their babies was demonstrated during the Lancashire Cotton Famine of the 1860s. As a result of a shortage of cotton supplies due to the American Civil War many women were without work and so stayed at home with their babies; in spite of the poverty caused by increased unemployment, the infant death rate actually fell at this time, proving the importance of maternal care for the survival of babies. In the 1860s there was public agitation against this 'sacrifice of infants' (high infant death rate) and the 1872 Infant Life Protection Act tried to make some improvements. The Act was largely ineffective, however, and it was not until the advent of the child welfare clinics of the twentieth century that substantial progress was made.

For the baby born in Victoria's reign, therefore, there was a greater chance of survival at birth and during the first vulnerable years than in previous times. But what, then, of the next years? How had the hazards to life and health changed as the child grew older? In most Victorian novels at least one of the characters suffers from chronic ill health or dies young, reflecting accurately the statistics which show that in 1851 the average age of death was 30; half-a-century later the average expectation of life had risen to 44 for men and 48 for women.

Emigration and immigration

The growth of population during Victoria's reign would have been even greater had it not been for the continual stream of emigrants to the colonies and to America. Many poor people looked for a solution to their problems in the New World. Thousands of families packed up all they could carry with them and left in the hope of finding a better life in the United States, Canada, Australia and New Zealand.

On the other hand there was also a great migration to Britain, mostly from Ireland, especially after the Potato Famine of 1846. The Irish families settled particularly in London and the industrial areas of Lancashire, Scotland and South Wales. In 1851, one-tenth of the population of Manchester and one-sixth of Liverpool's population was Irish, while there were 100,000 Irish in London and 250,000 in Scotland. The Irish immigrants were usually poverty-stricken when they arrived and were used to a lower standard of living than many of those among whom they came to live. They tended to swamp the unskilled occupations, were often willing to accept lower wages and were feared as likely strike-breakers. The Irish families accustomed to poverty in the countryside accepted terrifyingly low standards of squalor in the congested towns. Laws were passed, for instance, against keeping pigs in towns, indicating the problem of the Irishman's ingrained rural habits for his next-door neighbours in the towns.

Public squalor and public health

Although the advances in medical knowledge before and during Victoria's reign undoubtedly contributed to the fall in the death rate, there were still formidable problems arising from overcrowding, bad housing, lack of sanitation and polluted water supplies. The buildings were infested with rats and bed-bugs (indeed bed-bugs were so commonplace that as late as 1847

4 Taking a last look at England from the deck of the overcrowded sailing ship that is taking the emigrants to a new life (from *The Graphic*, 1869)

the firm of Tiffin & Sons advertized themselves as 'Bug-destroyers to the Royal Family'). Edwin Chadwick's report, *The Sanitary Conditions of the Labouring Population*, 1842, revealed a sorry picture of families living in cramped attics and water-logged cellars, crowded into damp, unventilated houses with no proper drainage, sewage disposal or proper water supply. He declared that disease was caused, aggravated and spread among the working classes by impurities produced by decomposing animal and vegetable substances, by damp and filth, and close overcrowded dwellings.

> When these conditions are removed, by drainage, proper cleansing, better ventilation and other means of diminishing atmospheric impurity. . . such disease almost entirely disappears. . . The formation of all habits of cleanliness, . . . is obstructed by defective supplies of water.

Chadwick deplored the unnecessary waste of life, and made elaborate calculations to prove that the loss of the value of the labour of a working man who died early was a much greater expense to the community than the cost on the rates of introducing the public health improvements so urgently needed. He estimated that the expectation of life for a baby of a working class family born in any one of the great provincial cities varied from 12 to 15 years.

Health and water

Smallpox had been controlled by this time by Edward Jenner's system of vaccination, but typhoid, jaundice and gastro-enteritis were still a serious menace, and in 1831 came the first of the four serious epidemics of cholera. The second outbreak in 1848/9

5 It was not possible to lead a healthy life in living conditions like these. A Glasgow slum in 1868; note the coal shed and outside communal lavatory

caused 53,000 deaths and in 1853 20,000 died, half of them in London. Some doctors suspected that cholera was a water-borne disease but many people were sceptical and it was not proved scientifically until the 1880s. Lack of sanitation and disposal of sewage was the worst evil. Prosperous households had cesspits under their houses, which were rarely emptied; there were estimated to be 300,000 of these in London. Poorer families shared an outside privy, or lavatory, the contents of which were carted away from time to time. When Joseph Bramah's improved water-closet was introduced, the cesspits filled up more quickly and there was a worse danger of infection from seepage into the leaky, wooden water-supply pipes. Water was taken in London from the Thames but sewers also emptied into the river; the stench was so bad that the water companies had to take their supplies from higher up the river.

In the 1850s the connection between sanitation, water supply and health was eventually established and big cities began to remove cesspits and install sewers connecting houses to the main drains. The old wooden water pipes were replaced by earthenware pipes and water supplies were greatly improved. There can be no doubt that these improvements led to a fall in the death rate. In London the rate had stood at about 24 deaths per 1,000 for the years 1847 to 1871. By the latter date the improvements in sewage disposal and water supply were completed and in 1873 the death rate was 22.5 per 1,000 and in the last ten years of the century it had fallen to 19.2. The Public Health Act of 1875 gave the local councils not only the power to make and maintain sewage systems and water supplies, but also the responsibility for appointing medical officers of health and health inspectors who dealt with cases of infectious diseases and organized the disposal of rubbish and the cleaning of the streets.

Advances in medicine and surgery

As well as these vital public health measures, which greatly decreased the danger of infectious diseases, this period also saw great advances in surgery. Until the nineteenth century very few operations were performed and those that were had to be done with a patient who was conscious, though sometimes made drunk with alcohol, who had to be held down by strong men. 'Laughing gas' (nitrous oxide) was discovered by Sir Humphrey Davy and ether by Michael Faraday in the early years of the nineteenth century, but the most effective anaesthetic was chloroform which was developed by James Simpson in 1847. Much more complicated surgery could now be undertaken. Unfortunately, while the operation was often immediately successful, the patient frequently died later from infection of the operation wound.

It was not yet understood that sterilization was important at operations. Doctors wore old clothes spattered with blood and

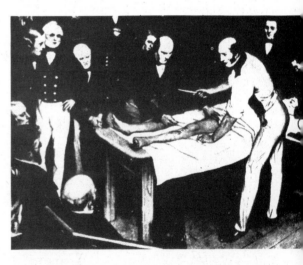

6 The British surgeon, Robert Liston, during the first operation performed under anaesthesia — an amputation done on 21 December 1846. In the background, extreme left, is the young Joseph Lister, who later became the founder of antisepsis

were not aware of the need to wash their hands or their instruments. The stench of surgical wards in hospitals was revolting and some doctors like Joseph Lister, in spite of resistance from colleagues, insisted on cleanliness, better ventilation and less overcrowding. However, Lister's instinctive demand for greater hygiene was proved to have a scientific basis when a French scientist, Louis Pasteur, published the findings of his research into the causes of fermentation in wine. He discovered that tiny organisms (microbes) caused fermentation and that similar organisms (bacteria) which were present in the air caused wounds to become septic. He went on later to prove that germs caused infection — one of the most important medical discoveries of all time.

7   Hospital Sunday — reopening of the Victoria Hospital for Sick Children, Chelsea, by HRH the Princess Louise in 1876. Lord Shaftesbury stands in the background

Lister developed antiseptics to prevent the infection of wounds, and though it took some time to overcome prejudice, gradually it became accepted that everything that came into contact with wounds — hands, instruments, dressings, etc. — should be sterilized. The number of deaths after operations fell rapidly and as surgery was now safe from sepsis, great new fields of surgical progress were opened up.

Towards the end of the century a German, Wilhelm Röntgen, discovered X-rays, which were to prove valuable in the diagnosis of disease. Doctors could now see inside the body and all kinds of surgery, especially the setting of broken bones, were improved. About the same time another German doctor, Robert Koch, identified the microbes that caused tuberculosis and cholera and soon after typhoid and diphtheria were similarly traced. In 1898, Marie Curie and her husband Pierre discovered radium which could be used to treat dangerous growths that the surgeons could not reach.

Radical improvements in the standard of nursing in hospitals resulted from the work of Florence Nightingale. After her work in the Crimea she published *Notes on Hospitals* setting out detailed plans for complete reorganization, and in 1860 she founded the first training school for nurses at St Thomas's Hospital, London. Discipline for the trainees was strict and as a result they became highly-skilled professional nurses. Other hospitals followed Miss Nightingale's scheme and by 1900 there were 64,000 trained nurses at work in Britain. Florence Nightingale also published *Notes on Nursing for the Labouring Classes* which at the time was nearly as popular as Mrs Beeton's *Household Management*. She urged in this the revolutionary idea that Victorian households should open their windows and let the fresh air into their homes.

Size of families

The Victorian period was the great age of English family life. In the 1870s and 1880s large families were customary among both the middle and working classes, especially now that so many children survived longer. The death rate fell as sanitary conditions in the towns improved and medical knowledge increased. In 1886, the higher proportion of births over deaths in England was 13.3 (per thousand), as against 10.8 in Germany and 1.4 in France.

The Victorian family often consisted of 10 to 12 children and formed a self-sufficient community, quite unlike the modern family of today with one or two children. For the working-class family with so many mouths to feed and low wages, it meant that mothers often went out to work and that children had to try and earn some money as soon as they could to contribute to the family's needs. In the middle-class family there was also the expense of three or four servants and perhaps public-school fees for the sons. By the 1890s there was some sign of the beginning of a reduction in the size of families among the professional and middle classes and the better-off working classes who were struggling to achieve a higher standard of living. However, parents least able to afford to rear children or to give them a good start in life still continued to have a large number of children.

8 A Victorian family, when large families were commonplace and not curiosities

2 'The Rich Man in his Castle, the Poor Man at his Gate'

Houses for the rich

During the nineteenth century the growth of population led to a vast building programme ranging from the dignified and spacious houses of South Kensington and Bayswater in London, and similar houses in the provinces, to the jerry-built, back-to-back dwellings of the Midlands and the North.

For the affluent, builders such as Thomas Cubitt and James Burton built hundreds of well-designed houses. These houses, of either stucco or yellow brick, with slate roofs, were built in a semi-classical style; somewhat heavy in appearance, they lacked the charm and lightness of the buildings of

9   Houses in Holland Park, London. They are probably now divided into four or five flats

the previous century. They were solidly constructed and many of them are still standing today. Most of the houses intended for single families with three or four servants were often four or five storeys high, complete with basements, and with impressive pillared porticoes. There was usually a small garden laid out with lawn and hedges of privet and laurel, in which the children could play, or sometimes there was a communal garden with a locked gate to be shared by local residents.

In the towns the houses were beginning to be built tall and narrow, because large houses were needed but ground space was expensive; in the country the houses could have pleasanter proportions and larger gardens.

Middle-class residences

For the less wealthy middle classes, houses of a similar style were built, but smaller, and in less fashionable suburbs. These houses were planned to be run with one or two servants. Paddington, Islington, Streatham and Brixton in London were typical districts for this kind of development as were the outskirts of developing industrial cities and market towns. These small Victorian houses were of brick and often covered with stucco; they were of simple, neat design with slate roofs and had a charming, cosy appearance. Mr Pooter's opening few sentences in *The Diary of a Nobody* by George and Weedon Grossmith describe vividly a lower-middle-class clerk's home in the suburbs:

My dear wife Carrie and I have just been a week in our new house, 'The Laurels', Brickfield Terrace, Holloway — a nice six-roomed residence, not counting basement, with a front breakfast parlour. We have a little front garden; and there is a flight of ten steps up to the front door, which, by-the-by, we keep locked with the chain up. Cummings, Gowing, and our other intimate friends always come to the little side entrance, which saves the servant the trouble of going up to the front door, thereby taking her from her work. We have a nice little back garden which runs down to the railway. We were rather afraid of the noise of the trains at first, but the landlord said we should not notice them after a bit, and took £2 off the rent. He was certainly right; and beyond the cracking of the garden wall at the bottom, we have suffered no inconvenience.

Later in the Victorian period a style of architecture known as the Gothic Revival became fashionable. It was doubtless a romantic reaction against industry and machines that made some people look back to medieval styles of building. As a result,

10 A Victorian extravaganza of a house including many historical styles and with an air of romanticism (about 1874)

turrets, towers, flying buttresses, spires, gables, oriel and stained-glass windows began to appear in public buildings and in large and small private houses. Instead of the neat, solid, early Victorian houses, over-decorated mock-Tudor and Victorian Gothic styles of infinite variety spread to the suburbs. This emphasis on ornamentation and decorative detail was echoed inside the house in the furnishing and fittings.

11 Frith's 'Derby Day' brings out the contrast between the lavish picnic being set out by a servant and the poor children looking on among the crowds on Epsom Downs

Houses for the poor
The contrast between the houses of the rich and the poor, and indeed in all aspects of their lives, was never more marked than in

Victorian times. Disraeli's novel *Sybil*, which he sub-titled *The Two Nations*, makes this point:

> Two nations. . . the Rich and the Poor. . . between whom there is no intercourse and no sympathy; who are as ignorant of each other's habits, thoughts and feelings as if they were. . . inhabitants of different planets; who are formed by different breeding, are fed by different food, are ordered by different manners, are not governed by the same laws.

And these 'two nations' were often barely a stone's throw from each other. The slums of London were pockets of squalor in the heart of the prosperous city. Behind some of the famous West End streets and squares were warrens of tumbledown tenements with dilapidated garrets, streaming cellars and no proper sanitation, the homes of tens of thousands of the very poor. Many of these buildings had been homes of wealthy people who had moved on to more fashionable neighbourhoods and the old mansions of the rich became the 'rookeries' of the poor. Seven Dials in London was an example of this and the Old City of Edinburgh was another. Sometimes these slums were the old homes of middle-class or artisan families who, as public transport had improved, had moved out to the suburbs and travelled

12 The crowded squalor of a second-hand clothing area in Seven Dials, London (depicted by Gustave Doré, 1875)

daily to their jobs in the city. Their old houses were occupied by several families. Growing up in a Victorian city slum was an unpleasant and hazardous experience. Mrs Gaskell, the author of many novels set in this period, describes a cellar which she visited in Manchester in 1848:

> You went down one step from the foul area into the cellar in which a family of human beings lived. It was very dark inside. . . the smell was so fetid as almost to knock two men down. . . The window panes were broken and stuffed with rags. In the thick darkness of the place there were three or four little children rolling on the damp, wet brick floor, through which the stagnant filthy moisture of the street oozed up; the fireplace was empty and black; the wife sat. . . and cried in the dark loneliness.

Purpose-built slums

In the industrial areas cheap houses were run up at great speed near the factories to give shelter to the rapidly growing population. There were no town-planning or building regulations so builders who wanted to make a quick profit built mile after mile of shoddy, insanitary dwellings that were soon slums. Families crowded into these hovels for want of anything else. Many of the houses were back-to-back dwellings. They usually had two rooms, the living room opening on to the street and with stairs from it leading to the upstairs room. There was no water laid on, no back yard and no sanitation except privies shared by many families. A report on the life of Staffordshire nail workers in the 1860s described broken window panes patched up with paper, nail-bags used to keep out the cold of the mud floor on which three or four children sprawled unwashed. . . 'In the corner a truss of straw, covered by a bag or two, is the bed of two or more little ones; no blankets, no sheets, no washing apparatus.' Children living in such conditions had no oppor-

tunities in the home or in the neighbourhood for a decent and healthy life.

A cottage in the country

Living conditions for agricultural workers were often as over-crowded and inadequate as those of town workers. The cottages might have looked picturesque from the outside, with thatched roofs and roses round the door, but inside they were often dark, airless and cramped. In spite of the large families to be housed there were rarely more than two bedrooms and often only one. An Official Report of 1843 described a two-roomed cottage in Dorset where the one bedroom contained three beds for the father, mother and nine children, whose ages ranged from a baby of four months old to twin sisters of 20. This was said to be 'not an extraordinary case'. It was reported that the stone floors of the cottages were 'wet or damp through the winter months and often below the level of the ground outside'. Sometimes refuse from the pigsties and the privies spread so that the cottages were nearly surrounded by filth and there were hardly any attempts at drainage.

But at least the farm labourers and their families had one advantage over the factory workers and miners; they had fresh air and the countryside around them. The country child's home might be a hovel, but unlike the poor child in the towns he could get out of his home into the open air and could enjoy the changing seasons.

A landlord's responsibilities

When Lord Shaftesbury inherited his father's title in 1851 he was appalled by the condition of the cottages on his Dorsetshire estate. His diary recorded:

> Inspected a few cottages — filthy, close, indecent, unwholesome. . . ; stuffed like pigs in a drum. Were not the people cleanly as they *can be*, we should have had an epidemic. Must build others, cost what it may.

13 The country cottage might look quite pretty from the outside but with its lack of amenities it was as much a slum as many of the houses in industrial areas (from the *Illustrated London News* 1846)

He was unfortunately deeply in debt and was embarrassed to inherit an estate 'rife with abominations', with things 'to make one's flesh creep', and to have 'not a farthing to set them right'. However he sold some family pictures and some land and was then able to build some new cottages and introduce some further improvements.

Better housing schemes for working people
Prosperous Victorians were aware of the housing problems of the poor and were afraid that the fevers and diseases that flourished in the slums might spread to their elegant town houses or comfortable suburbs. But intervention in this field was not yet seen as in any way a matter for government responsibility and it was therefore left to private individuals and companies to introduce improvements.

A very eminent contributor was Prince Albert, who designed a *Model Dwelling House for a Working Man* which was built and put on show in Hyde Park for the Great Exhibition of 1851. Each building consisted of four flats, two on each floor, with three bedrooms, a sitting room, kitchen, scullery, a meat-safe, coal bin, rubbish chute, and a water-closet with a flushing cistern.

14 One of Prince Albert's blocks of four flats for working people can still be seen at Kennington Common, London

The cost of each flat was about £120 which would have meant that they could be let at a profit for about 20p a week. *The Times* of 14 June 1851 described them as a 'good working model' and a vast improvement on many of the dwellings occupied by poor people which were 'a reproach upon our civilisation'. The visitor to nearby slums would be 'moved with compassion at the spectacle of such squalid misery' and would be grateful that the hard lot of those who toil in the lowest grades of labour had not been forgotten. A few similar blocks were built after the Exhibition closed but the number was tiny in comparison with the need. Unfortunately no one was willing to put up the capital to develop the scheme on a wide scale.

Hard-headed philanthropy

Octavia Hill, the grand-daughter of Dr Southwood Smith, the public health reformer, set about trying to provide some decent housing for the London poor in a very business-like way. She raised funds to buy working-class tenements, renovated them, and let them at reasonable but economic rents. She was not at all sentimental and was determined to help the very poor to raise their living standards by their own efforts. She recorded in 1875 what had happened when she gained possession of a tenement:

> Those who would not pay, or who led clearly immoral lives, were ejected. The rooms they vacated were cleaned; the tenants who showed signs of improvement moved into them, and thus, in turn an opportunity was obtained for having each room distempered and papered. The drains were put in order, a large slate cistern was fixed, the wash-house was cleared of its lumber, and thrown open on stated days to each tenant in turn. The roof, the plaster, the woodwork were prepared; the staircase walls were distempered; new grates were fixed;

the layers of paper and rag (black with age) were torn from the windows, and glass was put in; out of 192 panes only eight were found unbroken. The yard and footpath were paved.

Having put the tenement in order, Miss Hill kept an eagle eye on the tenants to ensure that standards did not deteriorate. She discouraged overcrowding by offering extra rooms to large families at a reduced rate. She organized the scrubbing of the passages and cleaning of the stairs, wash-houses and yards by the older girls living there. When rents were collected tenants were reminded if necessary about keeping their rooms clean, but any repairs needed were done promptly. Provided that they did not resent being so supervized, families in Octavia Hill's buildings lived a better life than those in ordinary working-class tenements and Miss Hill was even able to declare, 'the pecuniary result has been very satisfactory. Five per cent has been paid on all the capital invested'. Her scheme was a practical business proposition, not a woolly-minded charity.

In 1862, George Peabody, an American philanthropist, donated half a million pounds for the building of blocks of flats in London 'to ameliorate the conditions of the poor and needy of this great metropolis and promote their comfort and happiness'. Many large blocks were built with Peabody's money and decent accommodation was provided for hundreds of families. The Peabody Trust still exists today and provides housing for more than 20,000 people. Other companies such as The Improved Industrial Dwellings Company designed and built decent flats at reasonable rents.

A home of your own

Although many families were thankful to be rescued from the slums they often disliked living in flats and longed for a small house with a yard or patch of garden. Towards the

15 Peabody Buildings were rather forbidding barrack-like blocks but were soundly constructed and had reasonable amenities. This photograph was taken in Lever Street, Finsbury, London, in 1893

end of the nineteenth century, as wages rose and the standard of living increased, long rows of small houses for renting were built around London and all the industrial towns. The houses were small, with cramped rooms and, because of the size of families, tended to be overcrowded. However these houses were not too badly built and by this time (as a result of the Public Health Act of 1875 and other regulations) had water and gas laid on and proper drainage. Often they had fences round the small gardens at the front, and at the back, and they had privacy.

16 Small houses in Canning Town in the East End of London, about 1890

3 Home Sweet Home

Family life

Whether or not his home was an agreeable place depended to a large extent for the Victorian child on how well he had chosen his parents. This period saw a great upsurge of the middle class and with it a much stronger feeling of the importance of the family. The home became the symbol of prosperity and security, and the family man strove to have as big and as expensive a house as possible, filled with the grandest and most fashionable furniture and ornaments. The fortunate child from a prosperous home grew up in a large family where relationships between parents and children were clearly defined and rarely challenged.

The Victorian father was the undisputed head of the household and he expected unquestioning obedience, not only from his children, but also from his wife who had promised during their marriage ceremony to 'honour and obey' him. Wives frequently addressed their husbands not by their Christian names but by their formal titles, such as Mr Jones or Mr Robinson. Father, a rather awesome figure, was not seen very frequently in the home; he was usually away, working hard to make the money that provided his family with its high standard of living. When he returned his every wish was to be pandered to.

Mother, generally a gentle and somewhat sentimental character, supervized all domestic matters and was responsible for the day-to-day care of the children. However, for a great deal of her life between the ages of 18 and 45 she was usually involved in pregnancies. She therefore employed plenty of domestic help for the smooth running of the household.

Born into a wealthy home

Children from wealthy homes were brought up by nannies, not by their mothers. Nanny was often very strict and ruled the nursery with a rod of iron; her authority was rarely challenged and she had a great influence over the children in their formative years. The chief nanny to a family might have a nursemaid to help her and most of the time the young child would live in the nursery, playing there with his brothers and sisters. The nursery was usually at the top of the house well away from the parents' quarters. The children slept in a night-nursery nearby and it was Nanny, not Mother, who rose to comfort the child who was ill, or who cried in the night. Nannies in uniform took their young charges to get fresh air in the parks when the family lived in town, the baby sitting resplendent in one of the grand new perambulators of the period.

Many upper-class children saw little of their parents, and though they were well fed and clothed they lacked the parental concern and affection that is normally part of family life. Lord Shaftesbury, the social reformer, was neglected as a child by his family and ill-treated by their servants; it is recorded that he cried when he left home for the unknown terrors of boarding school, yet he also cried when he had to return to his unwelcoming home for the holidays. Most children, however, were taken downstairs

17 The Broad Walk, Kensington Gardens, in 1882. Note the nannies with their charges in perambulators in the right foreground

to see their parents each day, dressed in their best clothes and on their best behaviour, for an hour or so after tea. Children, it was said, should be seen and not heard.

Poorer families

It is arguable whether children from wealthy families brought up by nannies and servants were more fortunate than those from less prosperous households where the mother was directly in charge. As families were very large, the older children had to help look after the younger ones, though even in modest homes there were usually one or two servants to help. A child had to fit in with the hurly-burly of brothers, sisters and servants. He would not have much privacy but would be unlikely to suffer from boredom. An only child was felt to be very lonely and unfortunate. A family with a small income might employ a little waif from the workhouse and expect her to do the bulk of the household chores. However, there is no doubt that children of very poor families living in slums fared

worst of all. Such children had to look after younger brothers and sisters while both parents were out at work. They often spent the day in the streets, sometimes trying to earn a few coppers. Their houses were so dreadful that they could hardly be considered as homes at all. For these children family life was just a question of survival.

Furniture and fittings

Inside the affluent Victorian home the furniture and decoration reflected the outer appearance of the building. The graceful, elegant styles of the Regency period gave way to designs which were more substantial and cumbersome. The successful business-man wanted his chairs, sofas and sideboards to look grander and more opulent than the delicate pieces that had been fashionable earlier in the century. Solid mahogany and oak was preferred to the lighter rosewood. Whereas previous fashion had dictated a formal arrangement of individual pieces of furniture round the walls of a room, there was now a movement to fill the space with as much furniture as possible. The fashionable way was to put a great deal of the furniture in the centre of the room and at

22

**18 A group of slum children fending for them-
selves in the bleak streets**

various angles to the walls. Household possessions were the visible proof of the owner's prosperity.

Dining room chairs and sofas stuffed with horsehair and covered with a black shiny material made of woven horsehair were popular, though children often objected that the stiff hairs pricked when they sat down. There were also padded chairs and sofas fitted with coiled springs. Middle-class families had solid mahogany tables and sideboards and lots of small tables with ornaments on them. Most houses had a piano, as in the days before gramo-phones and radios a family that wanted to hear music had to make its own. The wealthy family would have a grand piano, a hand-some piece of furniture as well as a source of musical pleasure, while those with lower incomes and less space had an upright piano. A new invention at this time was the adjustable piano stool which spun round to the right height for each member of the family.

19 A Victorian family of about 1900 making its own entertainment round the piano in the drawing room

20 Victorian sitting rooms were cluttered up with a collection of furniture and ornaments. There were usually maids to do the dusting

Interior decoration

Dark colours were the most popular. Paintwork was often dark brown, wallpaper, curtains and furnishing materials crimson or bottle green. Carpets were usually of dark plain colours, and there was often a fur or patterned hearthrug. The walls were covered with pictures — water colours, oil paintings,

engravings, landscapes and portraits — and sometimes with china plates, pictures made from dried flowers, or embroidered pictures and samplers. In the drawing room, or parlour, mahogany newspaper racks and three or four-tiered stands, called 'what-nots', were used to display plants and ornaments. The bric-à-brac included china figures, paper-weights, vases, stuffed birds or wax fruit under glass domes, and articles in papier-mâché such as trays and boxes. As well as the large pieces of furniture there were lots of cabinets, bookcases, work-boxes and firescreens, possibly decked with covers. The chairs were provided with anti-macassars to protect them from the macassar oil which Victorian men used on their hair. The ornate chimney piece made of cast iron or marble was draped with a valance, fringed with bobbles, and its many little segments were filled with ornaments or family photographs in plush frames. The rooms were so crowded that it must have been very difficult for children not to knock things over.

The upstairs rooms

Bedrooms, from which light and air were kept out as much as possible, were furnished with solid, useful items. Some homes still had the four-poster beds with curtains fashionable in earlier times, but by the 1840s iron and brass bedsteads were the latest thing. They often had two mattresses on the beds, a firm one stuffed with wool underneath and a soft feather one on top. Later in the century, coiled-spring mattresses began to take the place of the feather mattress. As well as the bed there would be simple, roomy mahogany chests of drawers, dressing tables and wardrobes. There were few bathrooms in Victorian times but 'cleanliness was next to Godliness' and each bedroom would have a wash-stand with a china basin, water jug, soap dish, tooth glass and a carafe. Underneath there was often a footbath.

Bedrooms were not usually heated and so were very cold in winter. Beds were warmed either by a stone bottle filled with hot water or by a round, copper warming-pan with a long handle and hot coals inside which was smoothed over the sheets to warm them before people got into bed.

Lighting, heating and lavatories

Daylight could hardly penetrate the rooms of the Victorian house because of the long lace curtains that completely covered the large windows. Heavier velvet or patterned curtains hung behind them, supported by brass rings on a thick mahogany pole. Lighting was by gas or oil lamps. Gas pipes led to brackets on either side of the chimney breast and to a main light, often a brass chandelier, hanging from the centre of the ceiling. In the country oil lamps or candles were used. Electric light began to replace gas in many town houses in the 1890s.

Heating was provided by coal fires and there were grates in each room. Coal was cheap and scuttles had to be carried by servants from the basement to any rooms that were being heated. Fires were kept burning all day in cold weather in the downstairs rooms but were usually only lit in bedrooms in well-to-do homes or in case of illness. It was the excessive burning of smoky coal in wasteful but cheery grates that helped to cause the heavy 'pea souper' fogs which hit Victorian cities, especially London, each winter.

Bathrooms with full-length baths in Victorian days were rare. Prince Albert had the first bathroom at Windsor Castle installed in 1847 and they then began to appear in well-to-do homes. The upper classes accepted the need for a daily bath, but for middle-class families a daily wash and a weekly bath was felt to be sufficient. The baths were of painted cast iron with brass taps and set into a deep mahogany surround. Most people, however, used a basin or a hip-bath of iron or copper. The

water was heated over the kitchen range and carried to the bath by servants.

It was only during the 1890s that water closets became common installations in large houses. They were placed in the basement or in the yard outside the house. Earth closets, also outside, were more usual, especially in the country. To save the family from having to go out in the dark and the cold, night commodes or chamber-pots were used in bedrooms.

In the kitchen

The kitchen was one of the warmest places in the house because the cooking was done on a large cast-iron range in which a coal fire burned. The oven was on one side of the fire and on the other side was a boiler for heating water. The boiler had to be filled up with water from a tap at the sink and it was from this boiler that jugs of hot water were filled up and taken upstairs for washing or baths. Children loved to watch the cook or mother at work in the cosy kitchen on winter days but in the summer the basement kitchen would be a stifling place. Adjoining the kitchen was the scullery, where washing up and vegetable preparation took place. The servants lived and ate in the kitchen though they slept at the top of the house in the attics.

Domestic servants

It must have seemed to the servants in the Victorian household that the houses were designed to cause the maximum amount of work for the domestic staff who spent their lives walking up and down stairs with food, coal, water, or cleaning materials in the four- or five-storied houses. The wages of servants were very low although they received board and lodging. Even an office clerk like Mr Pooter in *The Diary of a Nobody* could afford to employ Sarah, a maid-of-all-work; she would be expected to work from six o'clock in the morning to nine or ten in the evening, with shorter

hours on Sunday and half a day off a week.

In an upper-class home there might be eight or ten servants from butler and housekeeper down to scullery maid and 'boots'. According to some contemporary novelists, children were sometimes rude and inconsiderate to the servants but this would not be common practice

Food

Just as conspicuous expenditure on houses and furniture emphasized the great gulf between middle-class prosperity and working-class poverty, so did the eating habits of the rich and the poor also present a startling contrast. Life for the middle and upper classes in Victorian England was very comfortable. Their incomes were not highly taxed, they could afford plenty of domestic help and there was an increasing range of new products on which they could spend their money. They went in for lavish entertaining, ostentatious tablewear, and ample, luxurious food. There were huge silver soup tureens, vast silver dishes for saddles of mutton and great sirloins of beef, silver wine coolers, bread baskets, large cruets, fruit stands and coffee-urns. There were damask cloths and napkins, cut-glass wine glasses, silver cutlery, finger bowls, and china by Crown Derby, Chelsea, Rockingham, Wedgwood or Spode.

A suggested dinner party menu for 12 persons in 1859 from Mrs Beeton's famous *Cookery Book* is startlingly extravagant to modern ideas:

Asparagus Soup
Turbot, Dutch Sauce
Vol-au-Vent of Chicken
Veal Cutlets
Leg of Mutton
Potatoes and Broccoli
Rhubarb Tart
Macaroni and Pine-apple
Nougats with Cream
Cheese Straws

21 This very grand Victorian bathroom would only be found in a prosperous upper-class home

However children were not allowed to partake in such delights and ordinary family meals were not of such a standard. Mrs Beeton recommended a more modest three or four course meal, such as 'Mayonnaise of cold salmon — Fillet of beef with vegetables — Currant tart'. The children usually had a hot midday luncheon and then nursery tea in the afternoon. A great treat was the arrival of the muffin man ringing his bell with his tray of hot muffins covered with a green baize cloth. Parlour maids were sent out into the street to buy his muffins and serve them for tea to the children in their cosy firelit Victorian nurseries.

22 The welcome arrival of the muffin man with his bell announcing that he has brought muffins for tea

The second half of the nineteenth century was a period when cheap imported food brought great variety and interest to the diet. Steamships and refrigeration meant that cargoes of meat, butter and cheese were arriving in increasing quantities from Australia, New Zealand and the Argentine. The prices of these imports were low and incomes were rising, so cooks and hostesses could afford to be extravagant.

Other new developments were the production of margarine, a substitute for butter, and the growth of many new food industries including biscuits, jam, condensed milk, chocolate, and canned fruit, meat and fish.

Nursery fare was, in fact, rather austere in comparison with the many courses and extravagant ingredients of meals for the adults. A streak of Puritanism was often applied to the children's diet for their own good. For instance, it was commonplace to insist on a child eating bread and butter first at tea before starting on anything fancy and even in comfortably-off homes children might well be offered *either* butter *or* jam with their bread.

Clothes and fashion

Clothes were yet another way in which the comfortably-off family could demonstrate its prosperity and its respectability. The Victorians were extremely fashion-conscious, taking a great interest in changes in design and up-to-date materials and accessories as described in the fashion journals. Paris, as ever, was the leader in fashion and the English magazines tended to copy French designs rather than to display original models. Mass production of clothes did not get under way until well into the twentieth century, so the new fashions had to be produced from patterns or copied from magazine drawings by women at home or by their dressmakers. Elias Howe patented a 'sewing-machine' in 1845 which used a threaded needle and a shuttle and produced a lock stitch. Soon most well-to-do families in Britain had one. In 1851, I.M. Singer patented his first sewing-machine and a revolution in the making of clothes had begun.

The revolution in spinning and weaving of the eighteenth century led to cheaper materials in Victorian times. The change to factory production also meant that women and children worked away from home and there was little time left for making their own clothes. Even the skills of patching and mending tended to be lost when girls and their mothers were employed for long hours in mills and mines. However, work made extra money available to buy ready-made and sometimes second-hand clothes. Cotton was now the most popular material and this made life much more hygienic as cotton clothes could be washed much more easily than the heavier woollens and linens of the past. Steam-driven sewing-machines were soon used in factories, and although elegant gowns for women were still hand-made many items such as under-wear, shirts and men's trousers were mass produced.

Baby clothes

Victorian babies were swathed in many layers of clothes. First a tight flannel binder was wound round the baby's tummy and nappies were put on. Then came a linen shirt, one or two long flannel petticoats and a linen petticoat. Next came a long dress of lawn or muslin with tucks or hand embroidery on the bodice. Babies' dresses might measure as much as a metre (40 inches) from shoulder to hem. If the baby was going out, a large flannel shawl enveloped him and sometimes young babies' faces were covered with a veil. A lace-trimmed or embroidered cap was worn indoors, and outdoors a cloth bonnet often trimmed with fur. It was believed that fresh air was harmful for babies so they were tightly wrapped up; they were prob-

23 This baby in its perambulator is dressed rather formally for a summer day's outing

ably more prone to illness through not getting enough good air to breathe.

As the babies grew older they still had to wear a lot of clothes. Since families were large it was normal to wear clothes handed down from older brothers and sisters. And as many garments were made by hand they had to last a long time.

A young lady's wardrobe

It was considered indelicate for girls in the early Victorian period to show any bare leg, so they wore pantalettes (thin trousers frilled round the ankles) under their dresses.

29

As they grew older, they wore shorter, knee-length drawers and a large number of underclothes including combinations (combining a woollen long-sleeved vest and knee-length drawers), stays made of a padded material, a chemise (like a long sleeveless blouse), a flannel petticoat, and for best occasions two or three cotton or muslin petticoats, the last one stiffened to make the dress stand out. Their dresses followed the fashions of their mothers and were full skirted, often revealing an inch of two of lace petticoat round the ankles. For everyday wear, fewer petticoats and plainer dresses of holland (a kind of thick linen) or woollen cloth were usual. Most girls wore an apron or pinafore. White stockings and black boots, either elastic sided or laced-up were worn, though in the house they were changed for lighter slippers without heels and often embroidered. For outdoor wear in winter, girls wore a pelisse (a fitted coat with cape or collar often trimmed with fur) and a fur-trimmed bonnet. No young lady would ever be seen outside without gloves; mittens were often worn at home in cold homes to help ward off the common complaint of chilblains.

During the latter half of the century girls followed their mothers' fashion for wider and wider skirts, made to stand out with stiffened petticoats. Ladies wore a wire framework called a crinoline and for special occasions a girl might have a crinoline of her own. Towards the end of the century however more sensible styles were adopted and some girls only wore one petticoat and a loose smock dress. Poor people, of course, could not afford the material for very full skirts and many petticoats and crinolines, but they wore long gathered skirts.

Although printed cottons with flower-sprigged patterns remained popular for little girls, dark colours or even black, were also quite usual. This was partly because of the custom of wearing black

for mourning. Once there was a death in the family, everyone, including children and servants had to wear mourning outfits. The high death rate, especially among infants meant that there were few families that did not have to go into mourning.

Clothes for boys

Little boys wore dresses until they were four or five years old when they were 'breeched' or put into long, uncreased trousers, which they wore with short tight jackets and waistcoats. They wore loose collared shirts with a 'stock' or bow. School-boys wore a peaked cap or a tall, crowned, silk top hat like their fathers. Later in the century when men began to wear three-piece suits, similar suits were made for boys. Tweedy, belted 'Norfolk' jackets came in for fathers and sons in the 1870s. Young boys were often dressed up in tartan kilts or trousers, especially after Queen Victoria's enthusiasm for the Highlands, and visits to Balmoral led to the royal children wearing tartans. Sailor suits, again favoured by the royal family, were very popular; they were made of blue serge or white cotton with square collared blouses and were worn with round straw hats with a name of a ship on the ribbon. 'Little Lord Fauntleroy' velvet suits with lace at the collar and cuffs, long knickerbockers and a plumed velvet hat became a craze in the 1880s following the publication of the famous Victorian 'tear-jerker' of that title.

By the end of the century clothes for boys had less fantasy about them though they were very formal. Younger boys wore short trousers, and a shirt and jacket while older boys wore long trousers or knickerbockers, a jacket and a stiff white Eton collar with a bow tie; both wore boots and woollen socks.

Getting dressed

Both boys and girls always wore some kind of head gear, even when playing on the beach or in the garden. In summer the hats were stiff, straw sailor hats; in winter they might be made of fur, felt or cloth. Dressing in the morning must have been a long and tedious chore. Many garments were worn and they were often very complicated to put on. Combinations had lots of buttons, there were rows of buttons down the backs of dresses and boots had to be either laced-up or buttoned-up with button-hooks.

The new look

By the end of the century, however, there was a new enthusiasm for open-air pursuits for both adults and children. Tweeds became popular and for girls the two-piece 'English' tailor-made suit became almost standard wear. School uniforms began to be adopted by some girls' schools. The uniforms provided a means of identifying the pupils of a particular school and were usually developed from drill or gymnastic clothes with the intention of reducing the weight and restrictions of normal women's clothing. In boys' schools the uniform usually consisted of striped trousers, dark jackets and Eton collars.

25 Even for the beach quite bulky sailor outfits, including hats, were worn

4 Children at Risk and in Trouble

A poor life

There was a marked contrast between the quality of life experienced by the rich and the poor in Victorian times. On the one hand was the ostentatious prosperity — not only among a small aristocratic minority, but also among a substantial middle class; on the other hand was the desperate poverty and squalid conditions of a large section of the working class. The poor were very poor indeed.

It was not until the nineteenth century that the state began to accept any real responsibility for the welfare of children and it did so at first very reluctantly. Even if a child were sick, poor, homeless, dirty, untaught, neglected or brutally ill-treated,

it was thought that this was the concern of his parents and not of anyone else. In the industrial areas the rapid rise in the birth rate was accompanied by a high death rate, due partly to a large increase in illegitimate births and the neglect, abandonment and even murder of some of these babies by their mothers. Many of the abandoned infants who escaped death through violence or exposure died as a result of the very bad conditions in the workhouses to which they were taken.

26 A London slum about 1889. There is a general air of depression and lassitude in these squalid conditions

In 1834 there was a radical change in the outlook towards and the official treatment of the poor. Change was needed, since the well-intentioned Speenhamland system, only worked out in the first place to solve the problems of some Berkshire magistrates, was widely copied and led to many evils. Among the results of this scheme of minimum allowances, whether a man worked or not, based on the size of his family and the price of bread, was the vicious circle of falling wages, dependence on charity and a high and rising poor rate. A substantial body of the working class, especially in country districts, through no fault of their own became paupers dependent on a weekly parish hand out. Thrift and independence were meaningless virtues and hard work brought no material rewards. It was even suggested that early marriages and over-large families were encouraged, because the allowances increased with the number of children.

The threat of the workhouse

The Poor Law Amendment Act of 1834 was a result of a Royal Commission set up to investigate the arrangements for the relief of the poor. The Commission's Report had revealed the degradation caused by an inefficient system that had flourished over a large part of the country for nearly 40 years. The new Act swept away the allowances and established two principles. Firstly, no able-bodied person or his family could any longer receive out-door relief. This meant that any destitute, but able-bodied, man (and his whole family) who asked for help were only offered one option, that of entering the workhouse. The second principle was that of 'less eligibility' which meant that the condition of any workhouse inmate should be less comfortable than that of the lowest-paid labourer outside. The most famous of the Poor Law Commissioners, Edwin Chadwick, summed up the whole idea as:

. . . making [the] workhouse an uninviting place of wholesome restraint, preventing any inmates from going out or receiving visitors . . . disallowing beer and tobacco and finding them work according to their ability; thus making the parish the last resource of a pauper (and making) the person who administers the relief the hardest taskmaster and the worst paymaster that the idle and dissolute can apply to.

One of the cruellest aspects of families having to go into the workhouse was the separation of husbands from wives and parents from children which was common practice. A writer in 1838 described how 'every poor man's family is liable, on the occurrence of some chance stroke of destitution, to have to their misfortune, bitter enough in itself, added the tenfold aggravation of being torn asunder and immured in the separate wards of a Poverty Prison'. Another described Chell Workhouse in 1842:

None of us wanted to go, but we must go, and so we came to our big home for the time. The very vastness of it chilled us. . . Doors were unlocked by keys belonging to bunches, and the sound of keys and locks and bars, and doors banging, froze the blood within us. We youngsters were roughly disrobed, roughly and coldly washed, and roughly attired in rough clothes. . . Then we parted among bitter cries, the young ones being taken one way and the parents (separated too) taken as well to different regions in that merciful establishment. I was hungry, but that bread! that greasy water! those few lumps of something that would have made a tiger's teeth ache to break the fibres off! In the afternoon we had our school work to do. . . If the devil had kept a school to teach boys how not to learn, he could not have succeeded better than that schoolmaster who asked God's blessing on the dinner he didn't share.

An M.P., Richard Oastler, wrote in a letter, 'a little boy, separated from his mother in a workhouse in Nottingham, raged in an agony of despair and actually tore off his own hair by handfuls'.

The standard of treatment of poor children in the workhouses seems to have varied widely in different parts of the country. Dickens' famous picture in *Oliver Twist* of near starvation and vicious discipline presents the dark side of the story while on the other hand there are accounts of workhouse children at Bolton being taken on annual expeditions to flower shows, on canal trips or excursions to Blackpool. At the Durham city workhouse 'cakes and fruit for all the children' were provided at Christmas. Sometimes children were housed with the senile women though in other cases the workhouses were run humanely with separate care for the sick and insane, no forced separation of children from their parents and cheap but cheerful school arrangements.

Innocent destitutes

The Poor Law Commissioners in fact saw poverty as something nearer to a crime than to a misfortune and therefore to be treated with harshness and not with sympathy. The able-bodied men and women were not the only paupers; there were also many more who could in no way be held responsible for their poverty — the sick, old, imbecile, widows, children, orphans and babies. The policy of deterring the fit but 'idle' poor from applying to the parish for help meant that the children without parents to look after them were housed in prison-like conditions with inadequate food and harsh discipline. Just as many adults would rather have died of starvation than enter a workhouse there were also many children who somehow lived on their own, by finding odd jobs and by begging and stealing instead of becoming 'children of the parish'. Joe, the crossing sweeper in Charles Dickens' *Bleak House* was such a case.

The problem of destitute and lawless children was an immense one. The ragged school movement tried to help neglected children who wanted to learn something. Children too ragged, dirty and verminous to be accepted in other schools were taken in. In 1850 it was estimated that 30,000 poor, filthy and lawless children in London were responsible for 95 per cent of the crimes committed. In 1865 a survey in part of Manchester showed that for every fifteen children between three and twelve years old, one was at work, six at school and eight were neglected. They were idling in the streets, tumbling about in the gutters, selling matches, running errands, working in tobacco shops, cared for by no one. In 1837, nearly 40,000 unwanted babies

27   Joe, the crossing sweeper in Dickens' *Bleak House*, said he 'didn't know nothing', as he had no one to care for him and had had no education except that of the streets (drawing by Kenny Meadows)

28 The Reverend Thomas Guthrie in his Ragged School in a church hall in Princes Street, Edinburgh, in 1857

were born. A Glasgow superintendent of police commenting in 1842 on the lack of care taken of children stated that in any large block of tenements he would be able to find 'a thousand children who have no name whatever, only nicknames like dogs'. In Edinburgh the usual answer of a child to 'when were you last washed?' was 'when I was last in prison'.

29 Ragamuffins from a London slum in the 1890s
(photograph by Paul Martin)

Childrens' homes and orphanages

After the 1834 Act some poor law authorities began to provide separate homes for children. Many authorities 'boarded out' children with families instead of keeping them in the workhouses; this was often an improvement for the children, especially if they were sent to the country, though inadequate supervision could lead to exploitation. Little schooling was provided for workhouse children.

On the whole the government seemed unwilling or unable to cope with these problems so it was left to individual reformers and voluntary organisations to take on the responsibility.

30 A meal at an orphanage in 1870. Charitable, wealthy patrons supported homes where orphaned and unwanted children were clothed, cared for and educated

The voluntary societies

During the nineteenth century a number of charitable societies for the welfare of children were started, most of them with a religious as well as a social purpose.

Thomas Coram had led the way in the previous century when he set up his Foundling Hospital in London. A deluge of sick and unwanted babies, often very ill, arrived at this refuge and a high proportion of them died soon afterwards. The Hospital gave up its function as a refuge for sick babies but

31 The original disused donkey stable in Hope Place, Stepney, where Dr Barnardo ran a ragged school and encountered Jim Jarvis, the first Barnardo boy

continued as a private charity which brought up and educated poor and orphan children.

A House of Refuge for Boys opened in Glasgow in 1837 and three similar places in London after 1846. These experiments grew into the National Refuges for the Homeless and Destitute Children (later known as the Shaftesbury Homes). The Church of England Society for Waifs and Strays (later the Church of England Children's Society) and Dr Barnardo's Homes were two more societies who took in as many orphan and pauper children as they could. Dr Barnardo had the motto 'No Child Ever Turned Away' over the door of each of his homes. His first home was opened in Commercial Road, Stepney, in 1867 and by 1905, when he died, 112 homes had been opened and 60,000 children cared for.

Other voluntary societies campaigned for different aspects of child welfare, for instance for the better protection of infants in workhouses and in the care of child-minders. The Society for the Protection of Infant Life pressed the government to regulate the activities of foster parents who were paid to look after pauper children. By the Infant Life Protection Act of 1872 such babyminders had to be licensed by the local authority. Infants' deaths had to be reported and a doctor's certificate supplied.

Voluntary associations also tried to help in the problems which revolved around the physical neglect of children who were beginning to receive full-time education. 'Puny, pale-faced, scantily-clad and badly shod, these small, feeble folk may be found sitting limp and chill on the school benches in the poorer parts of London', said a report in 1889. In the London School Board area 50,000 children were recorded as under-fed. In the 1880s and 1890s a number of charitable societies were set up supplying cheap or free meals, clothing and boots. The Fresh Air Fund and the Children's Country Holiday Fund took delicate children away for holidays. The Children's Happy Evenings

Association and temperance societies like the Band of Hope, tried to keep youngsters off the streets by providing some activities and moral guidance. Bodies like the Salvation Army and the Boys' Brigade offered drill and entertainment in the evenings. In the towns, hostels and homes for working boys were set up. A number of organizations like the Metropolitan Association for Befriending Young Servants, the Girls' Friendly Society and the Ladies' Association for the Care of Friendless Girls aimed at helping girls who were away from their families, whether in service or other occupations.

The view that a child was his parents' private property and that no one had the right to interfere was now being challenged. The National Society for the Prevention of Cruelty to Children, which had begun in a small way in Liverpool in 1882, combined with other bodies to demand government action. The Children's Charter Act of 1889 made neclect or ill-treatment of children a serious crime with heavy penalities; houses where ill-treatment was suspected could be searched and children could be removed from the custody of persons judged as unfit to care for them.

Steal or starve

It is not surprising that many of the neglected and destitute children in urban areas led a life of petty crime. Indeed, to stay alive many children had to beg and sometimes to steal. A case-study in Henry Mayhew's *London Labour and the London Poor* (1861) illustrates the point:

I was born at a place called Hadley, in Kent. My father died when I was three days old. I've heard my mother say. He was married to her, I believe, but I don't know what he was. She had only me. My mother went about begging, sometimes taking me with her; at other times she left me at the lodging-house in Hadley. She went in the country, round about Tun-bridge and there, begging. Sometimes she had a day's work. We had plenty to eat then, but I haven't had much lately. My mother died at Hadley a year ago. I didn't know how she was buried. She was ill a long time and I was out begging; for she sent me out to beg for myself a good while before that, and when I got back to the lodging-house they told me she was dead. I had sixpence in my pocket, but I couldn't help crying to think I'd lost my mother. I cry about it still. I didn't wait to see her buried, but started on my own account. I met two navvies in Bromley, and they paid my first night's lodging; and there was a man passing, going to London with potatoes, and the navvies gave the man a pot of beer to take me up to London in the van, and they went that way with me.

I came to London to beg, thinking I could get more there than anywhere else, hearing that London was such a good place. I begged; but sometimes wouldn't get a farthing in a day; often walking about the streets all night. I have been begging about all the time till now. I am very weak — starving to death. I never stole anything. I always kept my hands to myself. A boy wanted me to go with him to pick a gentleman's pocket. We was mates for two days, and then he asked me to go picking pockets; but I wouldn't. I know it's wrong, though I can neither read nor write. The boy asked me to do it to get into prison, as that would be better than the streets. He picked pockets to get into prison. He was starving about the streets like me. I never slept in a bed since I've been in London; I am sure I haven't. I generally slept under dry arches. I begged chiefly from the Jews about Petticoat Lane, for they all give away bread that their children leave — pieces of crust and such like. I would do anything to be out of this misery.

32 A boy from the London slums, 1860. Such a lad had to rely on begging or stealing to keep body and soul together

But most of these 'young Arabs of the city' did steal. Henry Mayhew described how the young thieves in the New Cut market, Lambeth, used to wait until dark before venturing out.

> In the evening, when the lamps are lit, they steal forth from their haunts, with keen roguish eye, looking out for booty. We then see them loitering about the stalls or mingling among the throng of people in the street, looking wistfully on the tempting fruit displayed on the stalls.

These urchins did not usually steal from the costermongers who were too quick for them but from old women's stalls and customers' baskets and sometimes in groups they rifled shop tills.

33 The start of a pilfering expedition, about 1900

Harsh punishment

In the early years of Victoria's reign crime was a grave social problem, made worse by widespread poverty and inadequate law enforcement. It was a time of violence and brutality. The death penalty was punishment for many offences ranging from theft to murder, and hanging continued to be held in public right up until 1868. Charles Dickens describes the barbaric practice which he felt exposed the very worst side of human nature:

> The horrors of the gibbet and of the crime which brought the wretched murderers to it, faded from my mind before the atrocious bearing, looks and language of the assembled spectators. When I came upon the scene at midnight, the shrillness of the cries and howls that were raised from time to time, denoting that they came from a concourse of boys and girls already assembed in the best places, made my blood run cold. . . . When the

two miserable creatures who attracted all this ghastly sight about them were turned quivering into the air, there was no more emotion, no more pity, no more thought that two immortal souls had gone to judgment, no more restraint in any of the previous obscenities, than if the name of Christ had never been heard in this world.

It is easy to understand that children who witnessed such dreadful scenes would

34 A public hanging at Horsemonger Lane Gaol. 'Thicker flocked the crowd apace, louder grew the glee, There was little kids a dancin', and fightin' for a spree' (*Punch* 1849)

develop a hard shell of callousness towards violence and dishonesty. Mayhew found that young pickpockets usually sprang from the poorest and roughest areas of London where their own family were often thieves by trade. They began 'to steal at six or seven years of age, sometimes as early as five years, and commit petty sneaking thefts, as well as pick handkerchiefs from gentlemen's pockets'. Many of these 'ragged urchins' were taught to steal by their companions in the penny lodging houses where they lived; others were coached by professional thief-trainers like Fagin in Dickens' *Oliver Twist*.

35 Oliver Twist being introduced to Fagin who trained a band of pickpockets and thieves in Dickens' novel *Oliver Twist* (drawing by George Cruikshank, 1846)

The introduction of a police force

A start had been made in policing London when Henry Fielding organized the Bow Street Runners in the mid-eighteenth century but it was not until 1829 when Sir Robert Peel set up a permanent police force in London that there was a serious attack on disorder and crime. In 1835, when local government was reformed in the boroughs, towns outside London were required to establish police forces. The 'bobbies' or 'peelers' were viewed with some suspicion at first but it soon became clear that for most citizens they made life safer and more peaceful.

Peel also managed to abolish the death penalty from more than 200 offences and though an orgy of crime had been predicted it failed to materialize. In 1844 children received much the same punishments for offences as adults. One in every 300 children between the ages of 10 and 20 was in prison mixing with adult criminals. There was much dissatisfaction with this situation. It was felt that there should be special treatment for young delinquents; they should be kept separate from adult offenders and emphasis should be placed on reform rather than on punishment.

Prisons and reform schools

The first separate prison for boys was built at Parkhurst in 1838. It was a distant fore-runner of our modern approved schools. Offenders who were too difficult were returned to the ordinary prisons but those who remained were to be subjected to 'a judicious course of moral, religious and industrial training'. Nevertheless the training should be hard enough to be 'a deterrent to juvenile offenders generally' though not calculated 'to harden or degrade'. There should be no comforts or indulgence which might 'weaken the terror of the law or lessen in the minds of the juvenile population at large, or of their parents, the dread of being committed to a prison'. Indeed the discipline to begin with included wearing an iron on the leg and a strongly marked prison dress, a diet reduced to its minimum and enforced silence during periods of instruction and duty. In 1840, however, leg irons were abolished altogether.

In 1854 the Reformatory Schools Act was passed and two years later over 50 voluntary schools had been opened. Discipline at the schools tended to be very harsh and some went as far as introducing barred windows, locked doors and cropped hair. The buildings were often inadequate, the food insufficient in quality and quantity, the clothing of poor standard and the children made to work too hard. Those running the institutions were confident that work was a virtue in itself, and that regular habits of work if engrained in childhood would ensure that respectable lower-class citizens would be produced. The Victorian reform school seems to our modern eyes a very severe and cruel place but at least its purpose was reformation not punishment.

Another long-fought cause for reform was that of putting children on probation instead of in prison. Pleas for this advance had been made as early as 1827 but it was not until 60 years later that the Probation of First Offenders Act was passed which enabled the young offender to be helped instead of being labelled a criminal.

36 Boys in the exercise yard at Tothill Fields Prison

5 Children at School

Education for the poor

Early in Victorian times most children did not go to school. Only about one in ten of the population had received any education and it has been estimated that half the people of London could not read or write. The Government did not yet accept responsibility for the education of the growing millions, though it had made a token gesture in 1833 by giving a small annual grant of £20,000 to be divided between two voluntary religious societies to help them run their schools. The grant was made to Andrew Bell's National Society for Promoting the Education of the Poor in the Principles of the Church of England and Joseph Lancaster's British and Foreign Schools Society, which provided a Nonconformist education.

Many people disliked the idea of the government grant to schools. Some had argued that there should be compulsory education but this was widely rejected as an attack on personal liberty. Some believed that the education of the poor was unnecessary and would only make them discontented with their lot in life. One of the reasons for 'the poor type of servant', wrote a correspondent to a magazine, 'is the very superfluous education given in our national schools leading many of the girls to sinful and criminal courses'. It was generally believed that everyone belonged to the

37 A rather idealized picture by T. Webster of a dame school with a nodding old lady in charge and very little equipment except a few books. Note the boy in a dunce's cap behind the teacher's chair

social class in which he was born; a few might rise in the world by great effort, but most were expected to accept their place as God's will. Education should, therefore, vary according to social class and should provide the learning needed for children to take up their appointed place in society: 'God bless the squire and his relations, And keep us in our proper stations' ran a verse of the times.

Types of school

As well as the voluntary church schools there were Dame Schools, so called because they were usually run by old ladies, often with little education themselves, but who were paid a few coppers a week by parents to teach the children their letters. Another contemporary verse sums up this kind of minding institution:

Where a deaf, poor, patient widow sits
And minds some thirty infants as she knits,
Infants of humble, busy wives who pay
Some trifling price for freedom through the day.

38   The Lambeth Ragged School for Girls in 1846

They were not very pleasant nor efficient places of learning, with few books, little to do and restricted space. In a House of Lords debate in 1861 it was said of these 'dames' in London, 'None are too old, too poor, too ignorant, too feeble, too sickly, too unqualified in any or every way, to regard themselves, and to be regarded by others as unfit for school keeping'.

There were also Ragged Schools, set up by some reformers to provide a little education for very poor children. 'They who are too ragged, wretched, filthy and forlorn to enter any other place. . . are invited to come here', said Charles Dickens, referring to Lambeth Ragged School. At first many of these schools were miserable places. Dickens described one in 1843 as 'held in a low-roofed den, in a sickening atmosphere, in the midst of taint, dirt and pestilence'. But Lord Shaftesbury and others did much to improve them and a few years later Dickens was able to comment on the same school that it was 'quiet and orderly . . . well white-washed, numerously attended and thoroughly established'.

There were also charity and Sunday schools which were mostly free. Their aims were to combat Popery (except in the few Roman Catholic schools) and to teach the children of the poor 'to keep their stations'. Reading and writing was taught, the Catechism was learnt by heart and some instruction in a useful trade was usually given. The alphabet was often learnt by heart in Sunday schools using the following religious rhyme:

A stands for Angel, who praises the Lord;
B stands for Bible, that teaches God's word;
C stands for Church, to which righteous men go;
D stands for Devil, the cause of all woe;
   . . . (etc.)

The quality of teaching

An official Report in 1818 commented on the 'lamentable deficiency in education for the poor'. Voluntary schools were confined almost entirely to the towns, and country districts were wells of ignorance. The poorest and least respectable parents often had a real desire to have their children educated but they were held back by poverty — either through lack of clothing or sometimes because the small wages the children could earn by going out to work meant too much to the family economy.

The voluntary church societies in receipt of government grants wanted to set up as many schools as possible and were in keen competition in providing an education from their particular religious point of view. Neither of them could afford to pay their teachers very much and so they both adopted and claimed to have invented the 'monitorial' or pupil-teacher system. It was not a happy method for the children. In quite large schools the one or two teachers instructed the 'monitors' in the next piece of information to be learnt. The monitors returned to their groups of about 20 children and did their best to pass on what had been crammed into them. Learning was nearly all done by memorizing things by heart and there might be little understanding. When children were tested they could often answer correctly if the questions were asked in exactly the order in which they had learnt the information; if the questions were asked in a different form or different order, the children were utterly lost. Discipline was very strict. When George III visited Lancaster's school at Bermondsey he asked how order was kept among so many children. Lancaster replied that it was 'by the word of command' as was the case in His Majesty's army.

39 The monitorial system in operation at the Ragged School, George Yard; St Jude's, in Whitechapel, 1859

An enlightened inspector

Having provided a little public money for the education of the poor it was clearly necessary to appoint inspectors to see that the money was properly spent. In 1839 a Committee of the Privy Council was set up to supervize schools receiving state support; it was fortunate that Dr Kay Shuttleworth, a great enthusiast for education for the masses, was appointed a secretary to the Committee. He suggested improvements for training of pupil teachers and encouraged the societies to set up teacher training colleges.

Dr Kay Shuttleworth was ahead of his times in his ideas of education. He deplored the fact that most teachers believed that 'education will be best promoted by coercion' and that 'knowledge is in itself repulsive'. He was sorry that 'the great majority of schoolmasters would conceive that they deserted their duty if they treated the children kindly'. The atmosphere in the Victorian schoolroom was not a cheerful one. The cane and the dunce's cap were

40 A Victorian village school. Note the teacher holding a cane and the children looking bored and anxious

standard equipment and the only decorations on the walls were tracts and religious texts.

Education and the government

In 1853 a great advance was made when a grant was payable for every child who attended school at least 176 days each year. But by the late 1850s the Government was hard up after the Crimean War and wanted to reduce public spending. By now the Government grant had risen to £125,000 a year and there were 21 Government inspectors. Some believed that the grant to education was not being well spent. A Royal Commission under the Chairmanship of the Duke of Newcastle was set up in 1858 'to inquire into the present state of Popular Education in England, and to consider and report what Measures, if any,

47

are required for the extension of sound and cheap elementary instruction to all classes of the people'.

The Newcastle Report of 1861 was critical of conditions in schools: 'The children do not, in fact, receive the kind of education they require'. Instruction was 'commonly both too ambitious and too superficial'. It was directed too much at the older scholars to the neglect of the younger ones who received no proper grounding in basic skills. Many children attended too irregularly to gain much benefit. The Report found the quality of the teachers greatly improved as a result of better training but declared that 'a large proportion of the children are not satisfactorily taught that which they come to school to learn' and by that they meant a firm 'grounding' in the 3R's — reading, (w)riting and (a)rithmetic. The Report saw no advantage in keeping the ordinary child at school until 14 or 15 but believed we should 'see the last of him, as far as day-school is concerned, at 10 or 11'. A member of the Commission had this 'bright view' of the possibilities of English elementary education 'floating before his eyes':

41 'The Three Rs; or, Better Late than Never.'
The Right Hon. W.E. Forster (Chairman of Board):
'Well, my little people, we have been gravely and
earnestly considering whether you may learn to
read. I am happy to tell you that, subject to a
variety of restrictions, conscience clauses, and the
consent of your vestries — you may!' (Cartoon by
J. Tenniel, *Punch* 1870)

By the time he is 10 years old. . . he shall be able to spell correctly the words he will ordinarily have to use; he shall read . . . the paragraph in the newspaper that he cares to read — with sufficient ease to be a pleasure to himself and to convey information to listeners, if gone to live at a distance from home he shall write his mother a letter that shall be both legible and intelligible; he knows enough to make out or test the correctness of a common shop bill; if he hears talk of foreign countries he has some notion as to what part of the habitable globe in which they lie; and underlying all, and not without its influence, I trust, upon his life and conversation, he has acquaintance enough with the Holy Scriptures to follow. . . the arguments of a plain. . . sermon and a sufficient recollection of the truths taught him in his catechism, to know what are the duties required of him towards his Maker and his fellow men.

Cutting the cost

These limited aims pleased those who wanted to prevent the waste of public money on education. Robert Lowe, now the head of the Education Department, introduced his ideas for a Revised Code for education in the House of Commons in 1861:

I cannot promise the House that this system will be an economical one and I cannot promise that it will be an efficient one, but I can promise it will be one or the other. . . If it is not cheap it shall be efficient, if it is not efficient, it shall be cheap.

His new system of grants was known as Payment by Results and it remained in force until 1897. For most children it was a nightmare. Grant to schools was dependent on pupils' attendance and success in passing an examination in the 3Rs.

The tests were given by visiting examiners who conducted one-day examinations in the schools. The grant per child was cut by one-third if he failed in one part of the examination and altogether if he failed in all three sections. Lowe's Code was certainly cheap — Government grant fell by £176,000 between 1861 and 1865 — but it was definitely not efficient. Teachers had to concentrate on dragging the slower pupils through the examination and ignored the bright children who could get through on their own. All interesting teaching was sacrificed to the basic 3R's and even religion was neglected as a non-grant-earning subject.

Enlightened reform

It is not surprising that the poet Matthew Arnold, who was an Inspector of Schools, reported in 1867 that 'the mode of teaching in the primary schools has certainly fallen off in intelligence, spirit and inventiveness' during the previous four or five years. The regulations which made 'two-thirds of the Government grant depend upon a mechanical examination, inevitably gives a mechanical turn to the teaching, a mechanical turn to the inspection, is and must be trying to the intellectual life of the school'. Nevertheless more children were at least obtaining the basic educational skills under the Revised Code than ever before.

In 1867 the Second Parliamentary Reform Act gave the vote to most male workers in the towns. 'I suppose it will be absolutely necessary to educate our masters', declared Robert Lowe. 'From the moment you entrust the masses with power, their education becomes an imperative necessity. . . You have placed the government of this country in the hands of the masses and you must therefore give them an education'.

But there were other reasons for further Government participation in education. The population was growing rapidly and there were too many children for the voluntary organizations to educate properly, even with some state aid. The industrialization of the country called for an ever-increasing number of literate and technically skilled workers, especially as our foreign competitors such as Prussia, France and the U.S.A. provided far superior public education services.

School boards and compulsory education

In 1870, the new Education Bill introduced into the House of Commons by W. E. Forster was a deliberate compromise. 'Our object', he said, 'is to complete the present voluntary system, to fill up gaps. . . not to destroy the existing system in introducing a new one'. School Boards to be elected by ratepayers were to be set up and run elementary schools wherever there were insufficient voluntary schools. The School Board schools were to be non-denominational and parents would have the right to withdraw their children from religious instruction if they wished. Parents would still have to pay a small weekly charge for their children's schooling though the School Boards could pay all or part of the fees for very poor parents and could, where there were sufficient school places, make school attendance for children between the ages of 5 and 13 compulsory. The London School Board did make attendance compulsory but it was not until 1880 that schooling was compulsory all over the country and not until 1891 that elementary education was free.

Life in school

Lessons in the School Board and church schools towards the end of the century were not enjoyable; indeed if a child enjoyed his lessons it was probably felt there was something wrong with the teaching. There were classes with as many as 90 children and 70 and 80 were common; two or three classes might be taught in one big hall. The only way to maintain any control was to have all the children doing the same thing at the same time. Children moved round

42 A London School-Board inspector and a policeman round up truants to make them attend school, in 1871

the school like squads of soldiers doing drill, marching in from the playground in single file and responding to blasts of the whistle.

Even lessons were treated rather like drill with commands such as 'Open your copy books! Take up your pens! Copy the sentence on the board!' Everything was very formal and mechanical, often involving a large amount of learning by heart and copper-plate handwriting. Stories were often religious in character or consisted of moral tales, and arithmetic tables were chanted by the whole class. Many schools did little other than reading, English grammar and arithmetic. If they did geography, it was only to learn facts by heart about the capital cities of the world, or the rivers of the British Isles in their order round the coast. History was a catalogue of names and dates; no attempt was made to teach sciences; music teaching was almost entirely singing songs learnt by heart, and only a few schools did any drawing or needlework. The only form of physical education was drill. Victorian children spent most of their time sitting up straight in rigid desks in class rooms. The class-work was mostly dull and uninteresting and the children were rarely encouraged to use their imagination or develop their own ideas.

Education for the rich

Richer people's children were usually educated at home by a private tutor or governess and then they might go on to a private day or boarding school. These schools varied widely in quality. There were a number of local grammar schools of ancient foundation, some of which by the nineteenth century had become famous as the public schools of England, attended by sons of the ruling class. There were innumerable private schools, for sons of the middle class, like Dr Blimber's academy in *Dombey and Son*, or at the other end of the social scale the outrageous Dotheboys Hall run by Mr Squeers in *Nicholas Nickleby*. For girls there were a few private seminaries.

Public schools

There were nine public schools at the beginning of Victoria's reign: Eton, Harrow, Winchester, Charterhouse, Shrewsbury, Rugby, Westminster, St. Paul's and Merchant Taylors'. These boarding schools were the preserve of sons of the gentry and their curricula were unchanged since the six-teenth century or earlier when most of them were founded. Little except Greek and Latin was studied. However many middle-class parents who wanted their sons to have a gentleman's education preferred a more practical syllabus and so were attracted by the wider educational programmes of such newer establishments as Cheltenham, Marlborough, Radley, Rossall or Wellington (founded between 1841 and 1853).

Life for the boys at the public schools in the early Victorian period was tough and hard. Augustus Hare recalled his experiences at Harrow in 1848:

> . . . how terrible the bullying was in our time. . . how little boys were constantly sent in the evening. . . to bring back porter (beer) under their greatcoats, certain to be flogged by the head-master if they were caught and to be (beaten) by the sixth form boys if they did not go. . . how, if they did not 'keep up' at football, they were made to cut large thorn sticks out of the hedges, and flogged with them till the blood poured down outside their jerseys. . . I may truly say I never learnt anything useful at Harrow and had little chance of learning anything. Hours and hours were wasted daily on useless Latin verses with sickening monotony. A boy's school education at this time, except in the highest forms, was hopelessly inane.

There was little organization or discipline in these schools but a system of sixth form prefects who ruled the school, using the younger boys as 'fags' (servants) and often indulging in corporal punishment and sadistic bullying.

Reform of the public schools did not come until the second half of the century after severe criticism of their primitive living conditions, brutality and lax discipline. Two reforming headmasters — Dr Thomas Arnold at Rugby and Samuel Butler at

Shrewsbury — led the way towards more civilized schools with more liberal education and moral purpose.

Mathematics, modern languages, geography, history and natural sciences were introduced into the curriculum. Dr Arnold aimed at training a boy to be firstly a Christian gentleman, and secondly a scholar.

Education, for Arnold, was bound up with religion and he hoped through his prefect system to influence the senior boys who would in turn imbue the whole school with the right moral atmosphere. We know a great deal about what it was like to be at Rugby at this time from the famous book *Tom Brown's Schooldays*, written by Thomas Hughes who was a pupil at Arnold's school. Arnold favoured the healthy competition of organized games, and Hughes gives us a vivid account of the special kind of football developed at Rugby.

43 The Lower School, Eton College (drawing by V. Starland)

Tom Brown's father's hopes for his son's schooling are clearly expressed: 'What is he sent to school for? . . . If he'll only turn out a brave, helpful, truth-telling Englishman, and a Christian, that's all I want'.

In 1864 a Royal Commission set up to investigate a handful of the leading public schools — 'the chief nurseries of our statesmen' — found them on the whole satisfactory though recommended less emphasis on classics and more on science, mathematics, music and languages.

Grammar schools

Below the great public schools were the grammar schools, many of them modelled on the public schools but some attempting to meet the needs of a wider public. These schools too had concentrated on the classics but now the range of subjects taught was greatly extended.

Education for girls

Apart from elementary education which was provided equally for boys and girls, the higher education of girls was very inferior. Girls were not considered very important and were sacrificed to pay for the expensive education of their brothers. After receiving tuition from a governess,

44 All spruced up in best bibs and tuckers for the photograph. Village school in Cornwall, 1900

perhaps shared with another family, they might be sent to a private day or boarding school. There the education consisted of little more than deportment and dancing, a little French and English, needlework, drawing and perhaps some arithmetic and geography, just the sufficient 'accomplishments' needed to make a good wife. However, many daughters were not willing to accept being treated as intellectual inferiors.

Frances Mary Buss who founded the North London Collegiate School for Girls in 1850 and Dorothea Beale who was the first headmistress of Cheltenham Ladies College in 1858, were pioneers in the education of girls. They profoundly influenced improvements in teaching methods and standards. In spite of the malicious rhyme against 'blue-stockings':

> Miss Buss and Miss Beale
> Cupid's darts do not feel
> How different from us
> Are Miss Beale and Miss Buss

there were a number of determined women and girls ready to fight for higher education. Soon the demand was for a university education and the chance to have a career in medicine, teaching and other hitherto male preserves. Girton College for women undergraduates was opened in Cambridge in 1869 and Newnham College in 1871: by 1879 Somerville College and Lady Margaret Hall had opened to women at Oxford.

6 Children at Work

Children in industry

In the 1830s thousands of children worked in factories, workshops and mines in the most appalling conditions, often for a mere pittance in wages. Their employers, the manufacturers who had successfully carried through a revolution in industry, resisted the demand for factory reform on the grounds that it would increase their costs and that it was an unreasonable interference with private property and individual freedom. It seemed that the prosperity of industrial Lancashire and Yorkshire depended on a few thousand children. William Cobbett made this point in the House of Commons:

> . . . a most surprising discovery has been made, namely, that all our greatness and prosperity, that our superiority over other nations, is owing to 300,000 little girls in Lancashire. We have made the notable discovery, that, if these little girls work two hours less in a day than they now do, it would occasion the ruin of the country; that it would enable other nations to compete with us; and thus make an end to our boasted wealth, and bring us to beggary!

But the employment of children was nothing new. Children had worked in the fields and in their homes, carding, spinning and helping in any jobs that they could do. No doubt they had often worked long hours and had sometimes been beaten for slacking, but working for one's parents or a local farmer was a very different proposition from working in a factory or down a mine. Children were exploited as cheap labour. They had to work very long hours in unhealthy and often dangerous conditions for low pay. Discipline was harsh. Parents were often loath to let their children work, but their wages were vital for the family.

45 Children working in a textile mill — carding, drawing and roving (drawing by T. Allom, 1835)

Factory work

In the early years of the revolution in the textile industry, when water was the source of power, the mills were built often in remote places near swift-flowing Pennine streams. Pauper child 'apprentices' were employed, who lived at the factories. However when steam power was introduced the textile industry concentrated on the coalfields of Lancashire and Yorkshire. Now the children employed were so-called 'free labour children' who lived at home with their parents.

The first effective Factory Act passed in 1833 forbade the employment of children under nine and limited the hours of work in all textile mills for children aged 9 to 13 to 48 hours a week. Four Factory Inspectors were appointed to supervize the carrying out of this Act. Two hours a day education was to be provided for children under 13 working in the cotton, wool, worsted and flax industries but this was found to be very difficult to enforce. Indeed it was hardly practicable to expect a child to be able to work eight hours a day in a factory and also be fit for two hours schooling, so later the government dropped this provision.

46 Girl drawing coal in a mine, often in passages only 45 centimetres (18 inches) high. (From the Report of the Children's Employment Commission, 1842)

Children in mines

In 1842 British public opinion was deeply shocked by the Report of the Children's Employment Commission which, after two years of gathering evidence, revealed barbaric conditions of work for children in coal mines. Children began work as early as four or five years old but usually at eight or nine. They started as 'trappers' sitting alone and in the dark for very long hours beside the ventilation trap doors, and opening or closing them as coal carts passed. Sarah Gooder, aged eight, stated:

> I'm a trapper in the Gauber Pit. I have to trap without a light and I'm scared. I go at four and sometimes half-past three in the morning, and come out at five and half-past. I never go to sleep. Sometimes I sing when I've light, but not in the dark; I dare not sing then. I don't like being in the pit. I am very sleepy when I go sometimes in the morning.

And Mary Davis 'a very pretty little girl' from South Wales said 'her lamp had gone out for want of oil. . . and rats or someone had run away with her bread and cheese'.

From about six years of age children began to work, pushing, dragging and carrying the coal from where it was hewn to the bottom of the shaft. Sometimes they were harnessed to the trucks like pit ponies and dragged them through the dark

47 Children being drawn up from a mine, 1842

passages on all fours. Some children worked the pumps and had to stand ankle-deep in cold water for as long as 12 hours at a stretch. In East Scotland it was reported that girls carried up to 150 kilograms (three hundredweight) loads of coal in baskets on their backs up and down rickety ladders beside the pit shaft. The children were often bullied and beaten by the miners. James Robinson aged 14 said he had been kicked, had his ears and hair pulled, had coal thrown at him but dared not complain as he believed the miner he worked for would kill him. His brothers aged ten and 13 had been beaten until they could hardly get home but dared not tell for fear of worse usage or in case they and their father lost their work. The excessively hard work in narrow passages often led to stunted growth and crippled or distorted bodies.

Danger in the pit

There was also the great danger of accidents as many mines had not even the most elementary safety precautions. For instance the ventilation doors, most vital safety-points, were in the sole control of small children. Boys were often in charge of the

winding gear whereby people were raised up or lowered down the shaft. Once a boy was distracted by a mouse and three boys travelling in the cage were killed; another time an inspector saw a child of ten hurled 56 metres (60 yards) to the bottom of the pit and dashed to pieces. There was the constant risk of falling coal or cave-ins, of being crushed by coal trucks, of suffocation by firedamp, of explosion and of drowning.

In Lancashire and Cheshire it was reported that accidents were 'a daily occurrence' in many mines and 'so common that a record of them is seldom kept'.

48 Girl with bare feet stoking a factory fire, 1871

The Mines Bill introduced into the House of Commons by Lord Ashley (later Lord Shaftesbury) passed without serious disagreement but in the House of Lords, Lord Londonderry and other mine owners criticized and amended the bill. 'Never have I seen such a display of selfishness, frigidity to every human sentiment', wrote Ashley in his diary. The Act prohibited the work underground of boys under ten years old and of all women and girls.

Reports and regulations

The 1833 Factory Act had applied only to textile mills and it was not until 1847 that regulations were made about the hours of work for children in some other industries. Many trades were, however, completely unregulated until well into the second half of the century. A Report of the Children's Employment Commission in 1843 described conditions in the calico-printing, lace, hosiery, metal, pottery, glass, paper and tobacco industries. It told of children as young as three years old working sometimes 18 hours a day, of exploited so-called 'apprentices', of deformity, disease and accidents caused by long hours and unhealthy and dangerous conditions. However, there were still plenty of people who saw nothing wrong in child labour. 'We would rather see boys and girls earning their means of support in the mill than starving by the roadside, shivering on pavements, or conveyed to Bridewell' (a prison) stated one writer on the factory system. Others commented on the sportive rather than gloomy appearance of the child workers, 'lively elves' whose work 'seemed to resemble a sport, in which habit gave them a pleasing dexterity'.

Many occupations for which children were used were much too straining for their immature frames. Brick-making for instance where they carried very heavy loads of clay on their heads for long hours each day was very injurious to their health.

A report in the 1860s on child labour in the Potteries revealed that some 11,000 children were working for as long as 16 hours a day for as little as half a crown (12½p) a week. Heavy moulds were lugged from the potters' wheels to the furnace where the temperature was about 54°C (120°F) by boys between six and ten years old. They were sent on errands from the great heat sometimes to freezing temperatures; it is not surprising that many of them died of tuberculosis and asthma.

Chimney sweeps

Even worse tortures were inflicted on the boys sent to sweep chimneys. The poet William Blake wrote:

When my mother died I was very young
And my father sold me while yet my tongue
Could scarcely cry 'weep, 'weep, 'weep, 'weep!
So your chimneys I sweep, and in soot I sleep.

These 'climbing boys' (and sometimes girls) were often bound as apprentices to chimney sweeps and were forced to climb the narrowest and most difficult chimneys in order to sweep the flues. They came back from their work at first 'with their arms and knees streaming with blood and their knees looking as if the caps had been pulled off' reported the Children's Employment Commission in 1863. They were driven in sheer terror of their masters up into dark, sooty places where some children got lost, wedged in or suffocated. They were urged up by threats, sticks, pins stuck in their bare feet or even fires lit in the grate beneath them. The climbing children began work at the 'nice trainable age' of about six and worked from 12 to 16 hours a day. Charles Kingsley's *Water Babies* made the plight of chimney sweeps like Tom known and Lord Ashley campaigned tirelessly for legislation to prevent this wicked cruelty, but it was not until 1875 that at last regulations restricting child chimney sweeps were passed.

49 A climbing boy-sweep had an unpleasant and dangerous occupation. This painting (by Baxter) was done in 1853 and it was another 22 years before this cruel work was made illegal

50 Much out-work was done by children and their parents for very long hours in their homes. This mother and daughter are making Valentine cards, 1875

Other work

Poor children in towns scratched a bare living from many kinds of jobs in Victorian Britain. Crossing-sweepers, boot-blacks, match-sellers, flower-girls, hawkers of all kinds and mudlarks all tried to earn the price of a night's lodging at a doss house or to have a few coppers to take home to their families. Mudlarks waded in the slime of the Thames in search of coal or anything else of value. Children also worked in many small workshop trades such as pillow-making and card-setting. The work in itself was not harmful but the hours were long. Girls employed in dress-making establishments, as lace-makers or glove-makers, had to work such a long day that it was common for their health to fail and many of them died. In the country children worked in the fields with their parents, especially at harvest and fruit picking times. Young children were employed as bird-scarers; older ones as goose-girls or shepherds, or to weed or to pick up stones from the fields. They might have to walk five or six miles to get to the work in the morning and then all the way home at night. Their wages were very low and the work they did was often hard and exhausting.

Domestic service

Apart from work in factories, workshops and mines the main other source of employment for girls was domestic service. At the Census of 1851 there were over a million domestic servants in England and Wales, and nearly two-thirds of these came from country homes. When a daughter in a farm labourer's cottage reached the age of 12 or so her family often tried to find her 'a place' as a domestic servant. It might be work in the kitchen of a small farmer or in a grand house. Whichever it was it was an exhausting life. She had to rise early and often got to bed late, the work was heavy and hard and the pay perhaps £3 a year. Her employer or the higher servants were supposed to train her but for her early years she was a drudge and many young girls were worn out by such service before they had completed their growth.

51 As a domestic servant, a girl would receive food and clothing from her employer, but her wages would be very low (drawing by John Leeds, 1843)

7 Children at Play

Divisions in society

The sharp social divisions that permeated Victorian life, to be seen in their housing, furniture, clothes, schooling and employment, were also marked in leisure activities. The unfortunate child who lived in a slum or worked in a factory had little time or money for amusements. Spare time in itself was a luxury. Only on Sundays, when workplaces and places of entertainment alike were closed, could the working-class child get some rest and perhaps some fresh air. The fortunate middle-class child, on the other hand, had plenty of time to enjoy books, toys, expeditions and even holidays at the seaside.

There was also a sharp division between town and country pursuits. In the country many of the old customs and festivals were still observed — harvest home, sheep-shearing suppers, Whitsun walks, tithe feasts, agricultural shows, markets and fairs. The annual fairs were often still 'hiring' fairs when farm labourers and domestic servants found themselves jobs for the next year. Improvements in communications made it possible

52 Brighton beach in 1888. Some ladies are bathing in the surf from the bathing machines and some children are paddling but everyone else is dressed very formally. The charge for sitting on the wooden seats was one penny per person

53 An Italian organ-grinder provides some entertainment in a drab street (photograph by Paul Martin)

for some country people to travel much further than in earlier times, and the progress in engineering technology brought bigger and louder steam-driven roundabouts and exotic sideshows to the fairs.

In the towns, the uprooting of people from their home backgrounds, the painful poverty, and the slum housing meant that there was much less communal recreation than in the countryside. Street-showmen such as organ grinders, Punch-and-Judy men, acrobats, street musicians and peepshows offered some rough entertainment for a copper collection. Street-traders selling ice-cream, lemonade, balloons, fruit, hot chestnuts, clothes, china or donkey rides tried to make a living and added to the interest of the dreary streets.

Toys, hobbies and games

The Victorian child had fewer ready-made or mechanical toys than children have today, and of course no radio, television or record-players, so he had to be more imaginative and inventive. As most families were large there was usually plenty of company to play with. Yet children were not allowed to be wild or noisy; parents believed it was their duty to be strict, and bad behaviour was punished severely.

On Sundays the family often attended church and the children went to Sunday school as well; many children were not allowed to play with their toys or read anything except 'improving' books on Sundays. It was a long, dull, boring day for such children.

Many toys given to Victorian children were beautifully made by craftsmen and some

63

54 A beautiful, carved and painted toy butcher's shop

have survived until today. Most nurseries had a large, strong, painted wooden rocking-horse with a horse-hair mane and tail. Carved wooden farm animals or a Noah's ark, dolls' houses with accurate miniature furniture, beautifully dressed wax or china dolls, wooden Dutch dolls, rag dolls, hobby horses, toy soldiers, musical boxes, peep-shows and toy theatres were popular well-made toys. Constructional and educational toys such as sets of building materials, alphabet bricks and clock-work models of steam ships or railway locomotives began to appear. Hobbies involving collections were encouraged by parents as educational pursuits — birds' eggs, butterflies, pressed wild flowers, shells and (after 1840) stamps. Girls would often fill scrapbooks with cut-out pictures from magazines. Some learned to knit or to embroider, and might make samplers which were pictures showing the stitches they could do, to be framed and placed on the wall. Card games like 'Happy Families' were new at this time and chess, draughts, ludo and dominoes were played. Parlour games such as charades, blind man's buff, consequences and forfeits were frequently played by the whole family.

Families often gathered round the piano

54 A beautiful, carved and painted toy butcher's shop

and sang together in the evenings. Girls of good family were expected to learn to play the piano and to sing. Dancing was also popular — the carpet would be rolled back and quadrilles, polkas, galops or schottisches would be danced with vigour.

Outdoor games

Wealthy and poor children alike enjoyed playing out in the open air in their gardens or in the streets. Hoops, marbles, whip and tops, stilts, see-saws, skipping ropes and rubber balls all had their seasons and there were hide-and-seek, singing games and all kinds of races and competitions.

Sports

Boys learnt all sorts of games at school and the rules of football, cricket and boxing were being standardized. Overarm bowling in cricket was thought to be dangerous and was not allowed until the 1860s. Cricket by this time was a national institution and was played on village greens throughout the country. The first Test Match was played in 1880. A lucky boy might be taken

55 Two little girls on a see-saw, about 1860. They are not dressed for vigorous exercise

56 These young Victorian cricketers pose seriously for their photograph. Their clothes seem to modern ideas more suitable for wearing to church than for playing a game of cricket

to see the great W. C. Grace play at Lord's.

Towards the end of the century the vogue for spectator sports began to grow. The Football Association was founded in 1863 and the English Cup competition began in 1871. At the 1901 Cup Final between Tottenham Hotspur and Sheffield United at the Crystal Palace there were 110,000 spectators. Rugby Union was founded in 1871 and the English League in 1888. Croquet was a popular game in Victorian times with championship matches played at Wimbledon. However from the 1870s tennis gradually took the place of croquet. Rowing was a favourite pastime and the Oxford and Cambridge boat race attracted big crowds.

One sign of the emancipation of women was that women and girls were beginning to participate in some of these sports — not only in the genteel activities of croquet and archery but also in tennis, golf, hockey and cycling. The straight-laced were shocked when girls went for cycle rides in 'bloomers'.

Books and magazines

There was an enormous growth in reading matter for children in the nineteenth century. Fairy stories and folk tales were very popular; Hans Andersen's tales were translated in 1846 and there were also Grimm's *Fairy Tales*, George Cruikshank's *Fairy Library* with alarming illustrations by the famous cartoonist, Ruskin's *The King of the Golden River* and Thackeray's *The Rose and the Ring*. Many books preached about the moral need to be good and to be charitable to the poor and it was not unusual to have sad death-bed scenes, as in *Eric or Little by Little*. *The Waterbabies* by Charles Kingsley, though an entertaining tale, also brought home the cruel plight of the little chimney sweeps. Lewis Carroll's *Alice's Adventures in Wonderland* and *Through the Looking Glass* were fantasies which soon became classics while Edward Lear's *Nonsense Verses* made families chuckle.

There was a great spate of adventure stories and historical novels for older children like Captain Marryat's *Children of the New Forest*, Charles Kingsley's *Westward Ho!*, R.M. Ballantyne's *Coral Island* and R.L. Stevenson's *Treasure Island*. In many families, stories were read aloud, and sometimes the grown-ups might read Dickens' or Thackeray's novels which were published in fortnightly parts in magazines. The next instalment of *Oliver Twist* or *Vanity Fair* would be eagerly awaited by all the family.

Comics

The second half of the nineteenth century saw a large number of children's magazines. One of the first was *The Monthly Packet* first published in 1851. Other well-known magazines included the *Boy's Own Paper*, *Boy's Own Magazine*, *Boys of England*, *Chums* and *Little Folks*. Cheaper 'penny dreadfuls', comics often featuring hair-raising and blood-thirsty adventures were bought by poorer children and liked by most children, though middle-class parents objected to them. *Chips* and *Comic Cuts* first appeared in 1890.

Going to a show

Theatres and music halls were usually too rough and boisterous places for children to attend. Sometimes, however, they might be taken to a pantomime or the circus for a Christmas treat or to one of the small, tented circuses that travelled round the country putting on entertainments with clowns, acrobats and animals at local fairs.

Magic lantern shows were a popular form of entertainment and often educational as well. A great variety of slides, hand drawn or painted until 1880 but after that produced by photographic methods gave a travelogue of the wonders of the world, portraits of

58 Coming away from a matinee performance of a pantomime at the Drury Lane Theatre, London, 1866

the Royal Family, flower studies or stories for children. Panoramas or Dioramas depicted battles of the Crimean War or a journey from Niagara Falls to London. The first motion pictures were shown to astonished audiences in 1896. Children would be unlikely to see the moving pictures at first as they were often shown in Music Halls, and cinema halls were not built until after the death of Queen Victoria.

Holidays

Until the nineteenth century, holidays away from home were exclusively for the rich, as most ordinary people had neither the spare time nor the extra money to make them possible. Most people, moreover, had never travelled more than a few miles — the distance they could walk from and return to their homes in a day. There were, of course, a few traditional days off for religious festivals and local fairs and sometimes when work was slack there was some enforced 'holiday' but with no pay to accompany it. It was not, however, until the revolution in transport had occurred that the city dweller could go on a day's outing to the country or the seaside. Trips by steamer from London to Margate, from Southampton to the Isle of Wight or along the river Clyde were a delightful and invigorating change from life in the towns. The coming of the railways especially increased people's mobility and soon Mr Thomas Cook and others were organizing cheap day excursions for parties who wanted to get away for a day from the smoke and grime and to enjoy fresh country or bracing seaside air.

Beside the seaside

For the middle-class family the annual visit to the seaside with its long bracing walks along the cliffs, its sandcastles, donkey-rides, shrimping nets and sea bathing became a well-established habit. Bathing was strictly segregated with ladies and girls keeping in a separate part of the beach even though they were elegantly covered. Bathing machines were pulled down to the edge of the sea with the bathers inside so that privacy was ensured. As few could swim the usual practice was to bob up and down in the shallow water while holding a rope attached to the bathing machine.

But for the working-class family there was little chance of a week or two at the seaside, much though they could have done with the break. Days off were days without pay, fares and lodgings were too costly, so the workers' families had to be satisfied with an occasional excursion at weekends or Bank Holidays. The Factory Act of 1850 stated that women and young persons were not allowed to work after 2 p.m. on Saturdays and, as it was not worth keeping the premises in operation with half or less of the workers, many factories adopted a Saturday 'half-day'. In 1871 the Bank Holiday Act gave England six Bank Holidays a year and most employers paid their workers for these days. By this time cheap railway travel and rising wages meant that many working-class families had a little money to spare and that a limited amount of travel was within their reach. The cheap day excursion became all the rage — much to the chagrin of many middle-class visitors who resented the noise and crowds caused by the day trippers.

59 Paddling at Yarmouth, 1892 (photograph by Paul Martin)

60 The traditional Punch and Judy show holds the audience entranced at Ilfracombe, in 1894

The new seaside customers with only a day to enjoy were not satisfied with genteel, middle-class amusements although everyone appreciated the Punch and Judy shows and the donkey rides. The day trippers liked loud brass bands, fairs, circuses, firework displays and such spectacles as boxing contests and balloon ascents. There was money to be made out of entertaining these families so there was a boom in providing picture postcards, souvenirs, funny hats, ice-cream, rock, and fish and chips. Many resorts had piers constructed providing a safe walk out to sea where fresh breezes and clear views could be enjoyed and refreshments and entertainment supplied. On the pier were peepshows, slot machines, drinks and often 'nigger minstrel' concert parties.

Holidays for all

Towards the end of the century the wages of some working-class families had risen sufficiently for them to be able to contemplate a week's holiday at the seaside, particularly in Lancashire where the mills closed in summer for 'wakes week'. Families saved up for a week at Blackpool or Southport and boarding-houses providing cheap but decent accommodation for working-class families began to flourish. Often a system called 'apartments' was adopted where the family bought their own food which was cooked for them by the landlady.

Although there were still thousands of families for whom even a day at the seaside or in the country was still an impossible dream, for a much larger number of ordinary folk a day's or a week's holiday was an enormous pleasure and something that at the beginning of the century could not have been contemplated by any but the wealthy.

Index

The numbers in **bold type** refer to the figure numbers of the illustrations